The Solar System

BASIC THEMES

What is the solar system? The solar system consists of the Sun and all the objects that are held by its gravitational pull, including the nine planets and their moons, asteroids, and comets. The Sun is a star, like many that we see at night. Each planet has its own particular characteristics. Some are relatively small and rocklike, others are larger and gaseous.

The planets and moons are moving through space. Everything in the solar system is in motion. The planets, asteroids, and comets circle or orbit the Sun. Moons orbit many of the planets. At the same time, the planets and moons spin or rotate. The motions of Earth and our Moon create natural phenomenon, such as day and night, the phases of the moon, the tides, and the seasons.

The solar system is so enormous, it's hard to imagine. The distances between the planets are measured in millions of miles. In order to better grasp the enormous distances in the solar system, scientists use Earth as a comparison. Earth's diameter (one Earth Unit, or E.U.) is used for comparing the size of the planets. Earth's distance from the Sun is one Astronomical Unit (A.U.) and is used to compare distances between planets.

ACTIVITIES

Grade 1

Name the Planets, page 8. Concept: Earth is a planet in the solar system.
The Red Planet, page 9. Concept: Each planet has its own characteristics.
   Students learn about one planet, Mars, and draw a picture of it.
Spinning Tops, page 10. Concept: The Earth spins or rotates. This creates night and day.
   Materials: flashlight, ball, tape.

Grade 2

Outta Space, pages 8-9. Concept: Distances in space are vast.
   Materials: measuring tape, paper.
Spinning Tops, pages 10-11. Concept: Earth, the Moon, and the Sun are all in motion.
Picture a Planet, pages 12-13. Concept: Every planet is different.

Grade 3

Outta Space, pages 6-7. Concept: Earth is a relatively small planet. Students learn about the relative sizes by drawing the planets to scale.
   Materials: large paper, string, ruler.
The Moon Cycle, pages 8-9. Concept: The changes in the appearance of the Moon are caused by the Moon's orbit around Earth.
   Materials: flashlight, two balls.
The Solar Family, pages 10-11. Concept: The solar system is made up of many different objects that travel around the Sun.

Forces

BASIC THEMES

Forces are pushes and pulls that cause changes in the motion of things around us. Things must be pushed or pulled to get them to move. Once they start moving, they continue to move until another force pushes or pulls them. We can feel forces, but not see them.

Friction is a force that slows or stops things. Friction happens when two surfaces traveling in different directions pull at each other on a microscopic level. This slows down and stops the motion.

Levers and wheels are tools that make it easier to move things. A machine is a tool or a combination of tools. The lever is a simple machine. When you push on the long end, the energy you use is concentrated in a much smaller arc on the other end. Your weak push over a long distance is translated into a strong push over a short distance.

Gravity is a force that pulls on everything all the time. Some forces can act on things without touching them. Gravity is an important example. Gravity is always pulling on things. Gravity pulls on a book on a table. The tabletop resists the pull and keeps the book from falling. When we weigh something, we are measuring the pull of gravity.

ACTIVITIES

Grade 1

Rub a Dub, pages 16-17. Concept: Friction slows things down. Some things cause less friction than others.
  Materials: marbles, cardboard, measuring tape.

Moving Machines, pages 18-19. Concept: A lever is a type of simple machine that makes it easier to move things.
  Materials: cardboard, ruler, small block, heavy book.

Grade 2

Friction Races, page 19. Concept: Wheels reduce friction.
  Materials: a drinking straw, wooden or plastic blocks.

Down the Ramp, pages 20-21. Concept: An inclined plane makes it easier to move something up and down.
  Materials: a marble, a paper-towel tube, 10 books, a yardstick.

Grade 3

Rub a Dub, pages 16-17. Concept: Water reduces friction.
  Materials: two blocks the same size, string, a tub of water.

Gravity: A Heavy Subject, pages 18-19. Concept: Gravity is pulling on things all the time. Different materials resist that pull to different degrees.
  Materials: string, rubber band, wire, clay, ruler, metal spoon for weight.

Beginning Chemistry

BASIC THEMES

Children experience chemistry every day in the kitchen. The ingredients we use in cooking are different substances with properties that we can observe. Although most chemistry occurs on the molecular level, there is much we can learn just by using our senses.

Physical change does not cause molecular change. Many changes that happen to ingredients in the kitchen are physical changes. When carrots are sliced, or flour sifted, the basic nature of the ingredients is not affected. When you mix nuts and raisins in a bowl, the properties of the raisins and nuts remain the same.

Chemical reactions involve molecular changes. Chemical change means that the atoms and molecules of a substance have combined in a different form. This will create a new substance, often with different properties than the original ingredients. Chemical changes are difficult to reverse.

ACTIVITIES

Grade 1

Mix Masters, pages 20-21. Concept: Simply mixing things together does not necessarily change them. A mixture that does not create chemical change is easy to unmix.
Materials: mixable foods such as raisins, peanuts, pretzels, cereal.

Gobs of Goo, pages 22-23. Concept: Adding water to a substance can create new properties that did not exist before. (The water and cornstarch mixture should behave like a liquid when you pour it, but feel hard like a solid when you touch it.)
Materials: cornstarch, water, food coloring, a bowl, a cookie sheet.

Grade 2

Mix Masters, pages 22-23. Concept: Mixing things together does not necessarily change them. A mixture that does not create chemical change is easy to unmix.
Materials: sand, water, clear jars, coffee filters, measuring cup.

Do the Dough, pages 24-25. Concept: Mixing ingredients with water can create chemical change.
Materials: flour, salt, warm water, mixing bowls, spoon, food coloring.

Grade 3

Mix Masters, pages 20-21. Concept: Some substances react with water by dissolving, a type of chemical change. Others do not.
Materials: salt, sand, water, coffee filter, jars.

A Fizz with the Friz, pages 22-23. Concept: Putting two substances together can create a chemical change. When baking soda is mixed with vinegar, chemicals combine, releasing carbon dioxide.
Materials: vinegar, water, baking soda, bottles, balloons.

Weather

BASIC THEMES

Air is all around us. We live at the bottom of a sea of air—Earth's atmosphere. Air is not visible, but we can feel it and see its effects when it pushes on things.

Weather is the condition of the air around us—its temperature, moisture content, and motion. The sun's energy is responsible for most of the activity we call weather. The sun heats the land and oceans, and warm air near the ground rises, causing updrafts and air currents. The sun's heat also evaporates water, which rises into the air as water vapor, a gas. When the warm, moist air rises, it cools. The water vapor condenses into water droplets, which form clouds.

ACTIVITIES

Grade 1

Floating on Air, page 25. Concept: Air is all around us. We can't see it but we can observe its effects on things.
  Materials: construction paper, scissors, paper clips.

Where Does Water Go?, pages 26-27. Concept: Heat from the sun evaporates water. The water vapor rises and condenses to form clouds.
  Materials: two shallow pans, measuring cup, water.

Grade 2

Weather Report, pages 26-27. Concept: We can observe a lot about the weather just by using our senses.

Where Does the Water Go?, pages 28-29. Concept: Clouds are formed when water vapor, a gas, is cooled as it rises. Students observe the water cycle when warm water evaporates from the bottom of the jar. It rises and hits the lid at the top, which is cooled by ice. This creates condensation on the inside of the jar, and the water falls back to the bottom of the jar.
  Materials: clear jar, hot water, ice cubes, plastic bag.

Grade 3

Charting Clouds, page 25. Concept: Certain cloud formations are more likely to lead to rain than others. Clouds can be classified according to their shape and color. This helps us to predict the weather.

A Lot of Hot Air, pages 26-27. Concept: Hot air rises.
  Materials: construction paper, scissors.

Seeds

BASIC THEMES

Seeds are one way that plants make new plants. Seeds are a form of reproduction for plants. In the same way that dogs have puppies or cats have kittens, daisies produce daisies and tomatoes produce tomatoes.

Seeds are formed by flowering plants. Flowers contain male and female parts. Pollen is produced by the male parts and must travel to the female part where ova are stored. The pollen and ova unite to form an embryonic plant encased in a seed. The part of the flower where the ova are produced becomes the fruit, which holds the seeds.

Seeds contain a baby plant. Seeds contain tiny plants. They also contain food for the baby plant to live on in its first few days. A tough outer coat protects the baby plant. Seeds can remain viable for many years. They will only sprout when they have found the right combination of factors such as water and temperature.

Seeds have many ways of traveling. Seeds must travel away from the parent plant. Some can float or glide through the air. Others are carried by animals. The food in a fruit such as an apple is not there for the baby plants. It serves as an attraction to animals who eat the fruit and deposit the seeds in other places as part of their wastes.

ACTIVITIES

Grade 1

The Grass Is Greener, pages 28-29. Concept: Seeds contain tiny plants and food for them. However, the baby plants can only live for a short while on the food in the seeds. Without sunlight they cannot continue to grow. Materials: beans, dirt or potting soil, plastic cups, pencil.

Seed Search, pages 30-31. Concept: There are many different types of seeds. Students compare different seeds they find in their environment.

Grade 2

Please Be Seeded, pages 30-31. Concept: Seeds contain a baby plant and food, but they need certain conditions before they will start to grow. Materials: beans, paper towels, plastic bags.

Flower Power, pages 32-33. Concept: A fruit grows from a flower and contains seeds. Often the remains of the flower can be seen at one end of the fruit.

Grade 3

Please Be Seeded, pages 28-29. Concept: Seeds contain tiny baby plants. Materials: beans, paper towels, plastic bags.

Design Your Own Flower, page 31. Concept: Flowers produce seeds. Flowers contain both the male and female parts of the plant.

Design a Seed Pod, page 32. Concept: Seeds must travel away from the parent plant. Some seeds float or glide through the air.

Ants

BASIC THEMES

Ants are social animals. Ants live in a cooperative society in which they rely on each other, have specific jobs, and communicate with each other. An individual ant cannot survive without the colony. Some other animal species are cooperative in some ways, though not necessarily to the same degree as ants.

Ants have different jobs. Ants in a colony have different jobs. Each colony has one or more queens, which are the only ants to have young. The queen is the mother of all the other ants in the colony. The other two main types of ants in a colony are the workers (who are female but do not reproduce) and the males. The workers specialize in specific jobs, such as repairing and building tunnels, searching for food, guarding the nest, and caring for the young. The males have one function—to mate with the queen.

Ants communicate with each other. Social animals need to communicate with each other. Ants primarily rely on their senses of smell and touch. They communicate through movement and by releasing chemicals that can be smelled by other ants in the colony. Without communication, ants could not cooperate in maintaining their colony.

ACTIVITIES

Grade 1

An Ant Colony, page 33. Concept: Ants are social animals that live together in nests. Each ant in the colony has a specific job.

Now Smell This, pages 34-35. Concept: Ants rely on their sense of smell to learn about the world and to communicate. Students experiment to see how keen their own sense of smell is.
Materials: peanut butter, apple, cheese, small paper bags.

Grade 2

Ant Antics, pages 34-35. Concept: Ants are social animals. Humans are also social animals that cooperate in order to survive.

Now Smell This, pages 36-37. Concept: Ants use movement and touch to communicate. Students pretend they are ants and experiment with communicating through movement.

Grade 3

Ant Antics, pages 34-35. Concept: Ants are social animals. They cooperate and depend on each other for survival. Students compare and classify ants with other types of social animals.

Ant Watch, pages 36-37. Concept: Ants' behavior is not random. Each ant has a job and a specific way of doing that job. Students observe ants to see if they can determine the type of job each ant is performing.

Habitats

BASIC THEMES

Many animals create or find homes. Animals create or find homes to gain shelter, safety for their young, safety from predators, warmth, a place to store food, or other essential needs. Some animals create their homes by building nests or dens, others find homes in caves, hollow logs, or the abandoned homes of other animals. Animals that build their own homes change their environment. Humans often change their environment radically. Some animals do not have a specific home or nest, but spend their time in a series of places within a larger area.

Animals live in neighborhoods—their habitats. Different animals need different conditions in which to survive. They find habitats that meet those specific conditions. Animals and plants living in a habitat affect that habitat and can change it over time. For example, beavers create a pond by damming a stream, then over time that pond can turn into a swamp and then a meadow as it silts over. Animals share their habitats with other organisms. All the animals and plants in a habitat interact and are interconnected. A change in one part of the habitat affects all the organisms in that habitat.

ACTIVITIES

Grade 1

Home Not Alone, pages 36-37. Concept: Many animals create or find homes.
  Materials: shoe box, paper, crayons, scissors, tape or glue.
Home Is Where the Habitat Is, pages 38-39. Concept: Like all animals, humans live in habitats we share with plants and other animals. Humans can greatly change the habitats they live in.

Grade 2

Home Not Alone, pages 38-39. Concept: Beavers build their own homes and create a new habitat — the beaver pond.
  Materials: small sticks, glue, paper.
Home Is Where the Habitat Is, pages 40-41. Concept: Animals live in specific habitats.

Grade 3

Home Is Where the Habitat Is, pages 38-39. Concept: Humans share their habitats with other animals, even in urban areas.
The Web of Life Game, page 41. Concept: All the plants and animals within a habitat are interconnected and depend on one another.
  Materials: cardboard, crayons, clothesline or rope.

Sound

BASIC THEMES

Sounds are vibrations. When we hear a sound, the nerves in our ears are responding to a vibration. Pitch is determined by how fast something vibrates. Volume is determined by the size of the vibration.

Sounds travel as waves. When sound travels through air, the air molecules at the source of the sound push the molecules next to them, which push the molecules next to them. This wave action is true in any medium that sound travels in.

We hear sounds with our ears. Our outer ears are shaped to collect sound waves and funnel them into our inner ears. When vibrations reach our inner ears, nerves send electrical messages to our brain. These messages are interpreted as sound.

ACTIVITIES

Grade 1

Zounds!, pages 40-41. Concept: Sounds are caused by vibrations.
  Materials: lids from pots or pans. For rattle—milk cartons, sand, pebbles, dried beans, etc., plus construction paper, crayons, scissors, glue, tape.

The Feel of Sounds, pages 42-43. Concept: We make sounds by vibrating air as it passes over the vocal cords in our throats.

We Hear with Our Ears, pages 44-45. Concept: The outer ear collects sound vibration and channels it to the inner ear.
  Materials: construction paper, glue or tape.

Grade 2

Zounds!, pages 42-43. Concept: Musical instruments make sounds by vibrating air.
  Materials: rubber bands, shoe box or other box top.

Now Hear This!, pages 44-45. Concept: We use sound to learn about our surroundings.

The Line Is Busy, pages 46-47. Concept: Sound can travel through other media besides air.
  Materials: paper cups, string.

Grade 3

Zounds!, pages 42-43. Concept: Sounds are vibrations. Changes in the vibrations affect the quality of the sound.
  Materials: a flexible ruler.

Make Waves, pages 44-45. Concept: Sounds travel as waves. Students observe wave action.
  Material: rope or clothesline.

Hum Drum, pages 46-47. Concept: Musical instruments make sounds by vibrating air.
  Materials: cardboard tube, wax paper, rubber band.

Digestion

BASIC THEMES

After we eat food, it is digested in our bodies. Chewing and swallowing food are the beginning steps of digestion. Food travels through our body and is broken down physically and chemically. Then our body can absorb the nutrients it needs for energy and to build new tissues. What the body does not need or can't use is eliminated as waste.

Food travels through the alimentary canal. Food travels through a long tube that goes from our mouth to our anus. The tube has different parts. Each part has a different shape and function. The parts are: mouth, esophagus, stomach, small intestine, large intestine, rectum, anus.

ACTIVITIES

Grade 1

Something to Chew On, pages 46-47. Concept: The mouth is the first step in digestion. Students examine the inside of a friend's mouth and observe the structures there.

It's a Grind, pages 48-49. Concept: Teeth begin digestion by tearing and grinding food into pieces. Students duplicate the action of teeth and saliva by grinding some raisins in a cup.
Materials: raisins, cup, plastic knife or butter knife, fork.

Grade 2

Something to Chew On, pages 48-49. Concept: Different teeth have different functions. Animals have teeth that are specialized for the types of food they eat.

It Takes Guts, pages 50-51. Concept: Food provides energy and the raw materials to build new tissues. People should eat balanced diets to help their bodies stay healthy.

Grade 3

It Takes Guts, pages 48-49. Concept: Food travels through the body in a long tube made up of different organs. Each organ has a different shape and function.

Think Small, pages 50-51. Concept: The small intestine is like a long piece of folded paper.
Materials: two pieces of paper, ruler.

Decomposition

BASIC THEMES

Living things decay after they die. When a living plant or animal dies, it begins to decay. Specialized organisms, often microscopic, begin to break down the dead plant or animal. Many types of plants and animals live in and feed on decomposing organisms.

Decay is nature's way of recycling. When a dead plant or animal decomposes, it releases nutrients into the soil. These are used by new growing plants. Animals and plants that promote decay perform a valuable function in a habitat. Growth, death, and decomposition are all parts of an ongoing cycle.

ACTIVITIES

Grade 1

What Rot!, pages 50-51. Concept: Mold is a kind of organism that feeds on dead organic material. Molds help dead things to decay. Students experiment with growing mold under different conditions.
Materials: bread, dishes, water.

Rotten Recycling, pages 52-53. Concept: Decay is a form of recycling that returns nutrients to the soil and makes room for new organisms. Students practice recycling in their environment by planning a recycling center.

Grade 2

What Rot!, pages 52-53. Concept: All living things decay, or rot, when they die. Rot is caused by bacteria that feed on dead organic material. Students observe rotting food and record the stages it goes through.
Materials: jars with lids, fruit, vegetables, and other foods.

Home in the Log, pages 54-55. Concept: A dead log is home to many types of animals and plants that promote its decay.

Grade 3

What Rot!, pages 52-53. Concept: Organic materials, or things that were once living, usually decay much faster than things that were never living. Students observe different rates of decay by making and observing a compost heap.

Old Mold, pages 54-55. Concept: Mold is a kind of organism that lives on dead organic material. Each type of mold grows on different types of food. Students experiment with growing different types of mold.
Materials: different kinds of bread, dishes, water.

Germs

BASIC THEMES

Germs are microscopic organisms that make us sick. A germ is a generic term for a bacteria, virus, or other microscopic organism that makes us ill. Colds, the flu, and infections are all illnesses that are caused by germs. Not all bacteria or viruses are germs. Some bacteria live in our bodies and are beneficial. Not all diseases are caused by germs. Some diseases are genetic. Others are environmental.

Your body has defenses against germs. We are constantly surrounded by viruses and bacteria, some of which are harmful. A germ has to enter your body and grow there before it can make you sick. The body's first line of defense against germs is the skin. Germs enter the body through cuts in the skin or through body openings such as the mouth or nose. Inside the body are other defenses, such as white blood cells, which destroy invading germs.

We can help keep germs from making us sick. Stopping the transmission of germs is an important way of staying healthy. Simple steps such as washing hands with soap and water can destroy germs and keep us from getting sick.

ACTIVITIES

Grade 1
Is It Catching?, pages 54-55. Concept: Germs make us sick when they get in our bodies. We can stay healthy by stopping germs from spreading.

That's Sick!, pages 56-57. Concept: Many symptoms we feel when we are sick are caused by our body fighting off germs. Students conduct interviews to learn some of the effects of illness.

Grade 2
That's Sick!, pages 56-57. Concept: When we're sick, our body is fighting germs. We can help our body fight the germs.

Staying Well, pages 58-59. Concept: Our bodies are generally very good at staying healthy. We can help our bodies stay healthy by developing certain habits.

Grade 3
Is It Catching?, pages 56-57. Concept: Our bodies are generally very good at fighting off germs. Through good habits we can help our bodies stay healthy.

Chicken Soup, pages 58-59. Concept: Cold remedies help our bodies relieve the symptoms of illness as our bodies fight off germs. Some home remedies, such as chicken soup, are actually beneficial. Students conduct interviews and compare different types of cold remedies.

The Desert

BASIC THEMES

A desert is an area with little water. Deserts may be hot or cold, but they are all very dry. Antarctica, one of the coldest places on earth, is a desert—there is very little annual precipitation. It does rain in the desert occasionally, but water evaporates quickly, leaving little moisture behind. Deserts are often places with extremes of temperature.

Some plants and animals have adapted to life in a desert. Plants and animals that live in the desert have evolved special ways of coping. They are good at conserving water and can go for long periods without taking a drink. (Some never have to drink.) They have ways of dealing with extremes of temperature, lack of food, and other hardships. Most areas of desert contain at least some species of plants and animals.

ACTIVITIES

Grade 1

Dry Up!, pages 58-59. Concept: Deserts are dry places that often experience extremes of temperature. Students apply their knowledge of the desert environment to plan a desert "survival kit."

Built for the Desert, pages 60-61. Concept: Desert animals have bodies that are adapted to living without much water. They must also withstand extremes of temperature.

Hide from the Heat, pages 62-63. Concept: Desert animals have many behaviors that help them survive, such as burying themselves in the sand during the hottest part of the day. Students observe the insulating properties of sand by measuring the temperature in a sandbox.
Materials: thermometers, sandbox.

Grade 2

Dry Up!, pages 60-61. Concept: Desert plants have unique adaptations that allow them to survive without a lot of water. Students explore plant adaptations by designing a fictional desert plant.

Built for the Hot Desert, pages 62-63. Concept: Desert animals have evolved unique shapes and other special adaptations for surviving heat and lack of water. Students compare and classify desert and nondesert animals.

Hide from the Heat, pages 64-65. Concept: Desert animals often find shade or create shade to survive the heat. They also bury themselves in sand. Students observe temperature differences in the sun, in the shade, and under the sand.
Materials: thermometers, sandbox.

Grade 3

Dry Up!, pages 60-61. Concept: It takes special characteristics to survive in the desert.

You're All Wet, pages 62-63. Concept: Water is necessary for life anywhere, including the desert.

Based on the award-winning Magic School Bus books by
Joanna Cole, illustrated by Bruce Degen.
Based on the Magic School Bus animated television series
produced by Scholastic Productions Inc.

No part of this publication may be reproduced in whole or in part, or stored in a retrieval system, or transmitted in any form or by any means, electronic, mechanical, photocopying, recording, or otherwise, without written permission of the publisher. For information regarding permission, write to: Scholastic Inc., Classroom Magazine Division, 555 Broadway, New York, NY 10012-3999.

Copyright © 1994 by Scholastic Inc.
All rights reserved. Published by Scholastic Inc.
Printed in the U.S.A.
ISBN 0-590-48771-X
2 3 4 5 6 7 8 9 10   25   99 98 97 96 95

Major funding for Scholastic's The Magic School Bus television project is provided by Microsoft Home, makers of a broad line of quality software for your home computer. Additional funding is provided by the U.S. Department of Energy and Carnegie Corporation of New York. Produced by Scholastic Productions, Inc. Presented on PBS by South Carolina Educational Television.
The Magic School Bus is a registered trademark of Scholastic Inc., © 1994 Scholastic Inc.